Skylark

Skylark

Poems

Mary Ann Woodruff

Cover and Interior Design: Kathryn Campbell
Author photo: Studio Vogue

Skylark
ISBN Print Edition: 978-0-9896563-0-6

Printed in the United States by Kindle Direct Publishing
Published in the United States of America by
Moon Day Press, Bellevue, Washington

For my grandchildren,
Rita, Kurt, Jamie, Tess, Alli, and Logan, with love.

"Skylarks sing while they fly,
flinging rhapsodies into the air."

Writing poetry has given me the same kind of joy
a skylark must have,
singing its heart out as it soars.

What you hold is a journal; may it sing to you.

Acknowledgments

Thanks to *Presbyterians Today* for publishing "For Jane Adams Spahr," in 1993 and to *The Angled Road* (Mount Holyoke Club of Puget Sound Writers, ©2016) for publishing "How I Got Here."

"For Bob," "Waking" (as "Bedtime Story"), "What's Wrong?" (as "Say Nothing"), "The Explorer and the Writer," "Pantoum for a Marriage," "Low Tide," "You Loved Me Bigger," "Wonder" (revised and extended from "Gratitude"), "She Wraps the House Around Her," "Music" (as "Holding an Infant"), and "How I Got Here" were previously published in *The Last of the Good Girls* (Moon Day Press, ©2013)

I am grateful to Judith Skillman, Judith Barrington, Janice Gould, and my professors in the University of Washington Writing Certificate Program for animating my love of writing poetry. Heartfelt thanks also to the Mount Holyoke College Club of Puget Sound Writers (Liz Burr-Brandstadt, Greta Climer, Mary Dicker, Jules Dickinson, Emily Dietrich, Lori Heath, Darla Kennerud, Elisha Maidan, Meghan Palmer, and Sue Swanson) for their encouragement and feedback—and especially to my editors, Emily Dietrich and Greta Climer, who have given so much time, talent, and humor to their midwifing of *Skylark*.

Finally, love to Mary, for everything.

Contents

LOVE AND HONOR

FAITH, FEAR, and FURY

WOMEN IN BLACK

LOVE SONGS

"*Prose equals words in their best order;*
poetry equals the best words in their best order."

SAMUEL TAYLOR COLERIDGE

"*The poet's job is to write the truth;*
and then to write the truth beneath the truth."

JUDITH BARRINGTON

FOR ALL THE SAINTS

The hymn, "For All the Saints," is frequently sung at memorial
services, at least in the Presbyterian tradition I know best.

For all the saints, who from their labors rest,
Who thee by faith before the world confessed,
Thy name, O Jesus, be forever blessed,
Allelulia! Alleluia!

The poems in this section are in memory of the saints in my family: my
grandparents, my parents, my aunts, my former mother- and father-in-law,
and my sister. (For a primer on who's who, see the Appendix: Family Tree.)

Skylarks and Coverlets

Skylarks sing while they fly,
flinging rhapsodies into the air.
I heard them one spring day
in southern France, sprawled
on a grass blanket shot with scarlet
mixed to gray orchard's edge
with premature Kalamatas—
a poppy-splashed hike set to music.

My too-thin father,
twisted to fetal curl,
whistled a long sallow sigh—
another—
and then no more,
transported on an opioid comforter
to another place
while my mother and I stared.

Now in our garden
you can actually watch,
between sunrise and noon,
velvet pods open in slow motion,
shaking out a crazy quilt
of red yellow orange poppies,
a patchwork fugue whose refrain
I taste as salt.

John Lewis Sparklin, My Father's Father

It's hard to describe him
without describing my father,
they were that much alike . . .
a fringe of white hair around bald heads, smiling droopy eyes,
walrus chins with a wattle underneath, somewhat stooped.
Dedicated tomato growers, fantastic meat carvers,
intensely curious about the world
and lovers of debate.
Both John and James were homeloving men
who cooked, laundered, knit,
could make or fix anything, and did—painstakingly—
and more than anything,
I remember the exact cadence and inflection
of the way they said grace:

> *Accept our thanks, our heavenly Father,*
> *for these and all thy mercies,*
> *use them for the good of our bodies*
> *and ourselves in thy service.*
> *In His name we ask it, amen.*

My father said John's mother told John
he should become a minister,
said it so often
he finally believed he had a call.
He left school administration,
something he loved,
to go into the ministry
which was more challenging.
I heard him preach once;
strange to hear my unassuming grandfather
declare the Word of God from a high pulpit.

My father, James, said
John preferred calling on people
to preaching. He often took his look-alike son
in the buckboard out to the country
to visit the sick and conduct Sunday vespers.
I imagine them having quiet talks on those rides,
James pestering his father with questions,
the love flowing between them.
When my father broke his arm
jumping over a hitching post,
it was his father who held him firmly
while the doctor set the compound fracture.

Philadelphia scrapple—the worst version of sausage
you've ever tried—and apricot nectar
come to mind when I think of this grandfather,
that and smoking in the bathroom with the windows open,
Mother, Jean and I, when we were in Delaware
for his funeral. It was an act of respect; we knew
he would never allow smoking in his living room.

> *Accept our thanks, our heavenly Father,*
> *for these and all thy mercies . . .*

Anna Rodriguez Sparklin, My Father's Mother

I never knew her.

I've been told
she was a dynamo:
she led the choir, played the organ,
taught Sunday school, checked on the ailing and,
had my grandfather not been paid to do it
and had it not been the early 20th century,
would have given as fine a sermon
as the preacher did.

I've been told
her father—or was it her grandfather?—
ran a banana boat from Cuba to the U.S.
She was born in New York City
of Hispanic and Caucasian parents.
She was petite, and her swarthy coloring
separated her from the chicken farmers,
sulky racers, and their tomato-canning wives
in lower Delaware, where she lived
with her parson husband and their family.
She who'd been missionary to Arizona Navahos
used all her persuasive skills on
my parents' wedding day,
talking my mother's father out
of his bedroom, where he had retreated
after declaring he had nothing
he wanted to give away that day.

I've been told
by my mother that Anna was warm,
welcoming to her and to outsiders.

Mother wondered if her "otherness"
made her extra hospitable to strangers.

Before I was a year old,
Anna put a hand to her forehead,
uttered a whimper and floated to the floor.
Stroke, they said.
She never said, ever again.
A week later she was gone.

Clarence Henry Melson, My Mother's Father

This is the grandfather
who stormed out of school in sixth grade
in a fit of pique with his teacher.
He became a surveyor who could tell you
the exact length of a hem, even where it dipped
and by how much, to a 32nd of an inch.

This is the grandfather who every day
wore wool plaid shirts, fired up the wood stove
to cook hot cakes for breakfast,
who lived alone on the farm
in lower Delaware where he'd been born,
to which he brought his wife,
in which they raised their daughters,
for thirty years after he lost his love.

He usually clenched a pipe in his mouth;
I remember his deeply creased neck,
I'd watch it from the back seat of the car,
itch to put my fingers into the cracks,
wonder what he did when he'd ask Daddy
to pull over so he could get out of the car
and disappear into the woods.

It was fun to visit the farm!
His prize dahlias grew along
the path to the outhouse,
chamber pots waited under each bed,
butter churn on the summer porch.
He'd saddle up Lady, the broad beamed mare,
for me to ride, my legs sticking straight out.

A hole between the bedroom floor and the living room ceiling
let not only the furnace's warmth but the adults' conversation
drift upstairs to where we were nodding off in our brass beds,
floor boards wide and creaking, splashed with moonlight,
air alive with the sound of crickets and country.

One Thanksgiving we went "down home" from Rochester
so Granddad, my uncle, and father could shoot game for the feast.
Our English setter, Fleck, who'd practiced "setting" birds in NY
but had never heard a gun, scampered back to the farm at the first shot.
My father, steely-eyed, stood between Granddad and my sister—
on the grass, sobbing, clinging to Fleck's neck—and insisted
that no dog of his would be shot for being gun shy.

Between visits, Granddad sent frequent letters to my mother.
They were fascinating to the granddaughters,
one long run-on sentence that always ended
With Lots of Love *Dad.*

This is the grandfather,
gruff and short of breath,
who always cried when we left.

Mary Simpson Melson, My Mother's Mother

Was it the egg thing
that silenced you—
you, daughter of a woman
who always used three eggs
when a recipe called for two,
living as a wife in the home
of a mother-in-law
who always used two eggs
when a recipe called for three—

Was it the egg thing
that silenced you?

*(My mother told me once she didn't remember much about her mother except that
she was pretty, quiet, and a good cook. I don't remember her either. Like my father's
mother, she died before I was a year old.)*

For My Father, James Donald Sparklin, in the Hospital

Rest now.
The lawn is mowed; the storm windows
carried up the sturdy ladder
and wrestled into place again;
all the apples have been harvested,
their sweetness spills fragrance
from peck baskets on the porch;
the fence, newly whitened,
marches smartly to the front door
to which you will never return.

Rest.
She can drive, balance
the checkbook, arrange
for chimney sweep.
Anxiously, your eyes search
the darkness for messages,
unfinished business to pass on
before it's too late—
your fingers tap the sheets
as though to pierce the recesses
for lessons still to teach.

Rest.
Your work is done.

First Mother's Day Without My Mother, Ruth Melson Sparklin, May 10, 1992

It's a cold, cloudy Mother's Day.
In church a friend sings
about how important mothers are,
and I feel the tears well up.
Let them come, I think, and they do,
spilling over, pooling in my glasses,
rolling down my cheeks, snot out my nose—
a tender mix of remembrance and self pity.

I mop my face, tuck away sodden Kleenex,
attend to the service. No one
noticed, I figure, and that's just fine:
my own grief, sniveling and precious.

Last May in France on Mother's Day.
we got the call:
Mother was in the hospital.
Not to worry, everyone said,
don't even think of coming to Rochester,
she would be so angry.
So we didn't, and when I did get home
she seemed fine when we talked
from Seattle to Rochester.
It had been three months since
my father died. She was busy,
wrapped up in clearing out the home
they'd moved to when I was two,
getting ready to move to an apartment.
I remember our visiting that new place
after my father died, her reluctance,
the way she froze at the door
of the empty dining room.

The last time I talked to her
she had dialed my number by mistake,
intending to call my sister Jean.
She'd lived in her apartment a week
and reported a triumph: that day
she'd managed laundry
in the coin-op machines downstairs.
And then she died, that night,
with no warning, no cry for help.
No anything, except her minister
on the phone the next morning:
Mom's gone to the kingdom.
A broken heart.

How could she die, just like that?
No chance to say *I love you,*
to hear again, *you'll be OK.*
Today, I remembered all those times
reaching across the country to say
I fell off my bicycle, broke my arm,
had a miscarriage,
found a lump,
expected a baby,
saw my first tufted titmouse,
sent my last child off to school,
wrecked the car.

I guess Hallmark must make a mint,
and so does Ma Bell
on Mother's Day—
I think the Kleenex people
are doing all right too.

Lilacs

I hadn't noticed
a bouquet in that office,
but suddenly
fragrance poured over me,
and caught in my throat—

Our backyard hedge,
tiny clusters of purple pin points
one week,
luscious lavendar perfumed armloads
the next,
bouquets every spring on the hall table.

I strolled Highland Park with my parents
when my father could still walk.
Lilacs from all over the world flung
color and spice into our senses.
We were delighted, as veterans,
that we avoided the crush of Lilac Sunday.
We lingered by the enormous pansy bed
before we left.

Last year,
I drove my mother through the park
repeating our springtime ritual in silence.
We were early—
or was it late?—
for the peak of lilac blossoms.
We spotted the pansy bed
but did not leave the car.

Today
one whiff
flooded years through me—
oh, Mother,
can you smell them too?

My Father's Sisters

First came Dorothy, responsible, soft,
easy with company and cooking for them.
She and Uncle Ray had three sons
and a daughter. They lived in Selbyville,
in a big white house with a wrap-around porch and
Lucky, an enormous Chesapeake Bay Retriever.
They had a beach house at Ocean City, Maryland,
right on the boardwalk; the slamming
surf kept us awake at night.
They owned a chicken farm and race horses,
sulky-pulling pacers and trotters that ran
summer nights at the Harrington Race Track.
Ray had rheumatoid arthritis. He and Dorothy
went anywhere a cure might be had, with no luck.

Next, before my father, came Edith,
a curly blond independent spirit.
Edith, a nurse, went to Labrador
with the Grenfell mission, providing
all sorts of medical care from an
isolated clinic. On her return, she
was nurse for Sammy DuPont, who later,
as Pete, became governor of Delaware.
She and my dad were always close:
the drinkers in their teetotaling family,
they'd laugh. Edith married late and
took up weaving before she died
in a lovely Greenfield Village cottage
near the Dearborn Inn Uncle Dick managed.

Finally came Virginia, the sober
high school English teacher who

most resembled her mother—
small, dark eyed and always in motion.
Virginia never married, but kept
home for her parson father
in a row house in Wilmington.
She kept a closet full of games
for visiting granddaughters,
and frequent admonishments
for her siblings. "I already had a
mother," my father once sputtered.
Her letters always ended predictably:
"Hope you are keeping well."

Margaret Melson Edgell, My Mother's Sister

Aunt Margaret
was younger than my mother
by three years. She was the one who stayed
in Delaware, married to Uncle Louis,
who built sewers and roads in Delaware
and Maryland, while my mother moved
to Rochester with my sister and father for his job
as sales engineer for a machine tool company.

Aunt Margaret
was a great cook;
her scrambled eggs were the best.
She had a delightful Southern accent Mother
always adopted for a few weeks after we'd visited.
She was the mother of my favorite cousin Jane,
just my age, and a younger son, Bob.
She was cheerful, chatty, with a ready laugh—
I can still hear the two sisters talking,
remembering friends by their maiden names,
staying up late with their memories ("My land, Ruth!")
while Jane and I nestled into her bed on Lewes Beach.
They had long phone calls between visits.

Aunt Margaret,
though I never saw any of it, suffered
from depression—serious depression.
I don't know how many times she had
electroshock treatments, but she would disappear,
be "away" for a while, Mother would say, and
when she came back, she was subdued, forgetful.
Aunt Margaret yoyoed between treatments
and stability for years. Sometimes
she and Mother weren't speaking.

Aunt Margaret
was tall, lithe. She and my sister
were similar in build and looked alike,
we thought. Both Margaret and Ruth
had portraits done as children;
I found a picture of Mother's portrait
recently, and it looks just like Jane.
Family ran through all of us, it's fair to say.
Sometimes I've wondered if depression
hasn't run through all of us as well.

Hoke Smith Woodruff, My Former Father-in-Law

Don't ask him why the grass is green
unless you have time
for a lengthy discourse
on chlorophyll
and photosynthesis.

Do call Hoke
if your child dies
in the middle of the night.
He's the one you'll want there first,
he and his quiet, solid,
compassionate presence.

Edna Baker Woodruff, My Former Mother-in-Law

She woke every day wondering,
"What funny thing will happen today?"
Something funny always did:
she created it.
Just ask Sally Campbell
about her night with Eddie
in a Vancover hotel
waiting for the roll-away.

As a mother-in-law she never
offered advice.
But if you asked for it,
she let you have it,
straight.

Sisters (2017 Christmas Poem for my sister, Jean Sparklin Hager)

They have known each other
longer than anyone;
they have history, ancestors,
relatives in common.
Many they even like.

They talk often—
though not often enough—
laughing, lamenting,
finishing each other's sentences.
They pray for their families.

They anchor the coasts,
their kids are East and West;
still, their politics are similar,
their anguish often the same.
What can we do about—fill in the blank.

Every so often
they are together for real—
hours to share, nourished by
food, drink, pride, and love.
They marvel at the next generations.

Now they anticipate a reunion
by the sea they swam as girls,
sharing their history with family,
and precious time again with each other.
No friendship like this one.

*(The Bethany Beach family reunion, July, 2018, celebrating Jean's eighty-fifth and
my eightieth birthdays, was held without Jean. Diagnosed with lung cancer a month
earlier, she stayed home and died a week after our get together.)*

What These Saints Are to Me

We are a family of storytellers.
I want my grandchildren
to have these stories, long after
there's anyone who can tell them
from real knowledge,
anyone who can add life and color
to a hint on Ancestry.com.

We carry a torch for our ancesters,
evoke their memories
hoping their good qualities
are not extinguished, that even we
carry them onward in our lives
lest they be lost to a world
needing goodness and light.

We search ourselves
and our children
to see who resembles whom:
Who got the talent for music?
Who the quick sense of humor?
Who that gentle, reassuring presence?
Who the love of handicraft?

What are all these saints to me?
Mirrors in which I see myself,
my children, my grandchildren,
and perhaps a glimpse of the future;
memories with which I warm my heart;
miracles of happenstance
that nourish a family tree.

LOVE AND HONOR

Not everyone has the good fortune to find two wonderful people to love deeply. I have. My first marriage to Bob Woodruff was steeped in the joy of early love and growing family. Challenges to our marriage and changes in us eventually muddled that joy. And then—Mary Dispenza. Finding, loving, nearly losing, and finally committing to the woman who is now my wife meant finding and honoring my self. All of this is well documented in *The Last of the Good Girls*, © 2013, Moon Day Press.

Here is more of the story, in poem.

For Bob, 1970

We round a bend in the road
and there is a scene so splendid we catch our breath—
and I enjoy it because it presents an exercise in description,
    and I mentally poetize the azure sky,
      the sparkling foliage—
and you enjoy it.

We walk hand in hand through a forest,
pine scented sunlight filtering through the trees—
and I enjoy it because I've brought this great book along
    so we can identify wild flowers
    and classify ferns—
 and you enjoy it.

We sit beneath Ravinia's star-speckled canopy
while dancers swirl their colors before us
and fireflies glitter just out of range—
and I enjoy it because I'm following the melodic theme
    from instrument to instrument
    and picking out social satire, intended or not—
and you enjoy it.

I don't know how you got this way,
how you embrace life with such zest and naturalness,
how you enjoy it without description, classification,
    analysis or explanation,
    but I know you do—
and I enjoy it.

Bedtime on Coe Road

Has anybody seen my mouse?

Three bodies drop to the floor,
three butts up, three sets of eyes
scan beneath the bed,
three voices, one deep, cry plaintively,
I opened the box for half a minute . . .
Just to make sure he was really in it.
And while I was looking, he jumped outside.
I tried to catch him, I tried I tried . . .
Has anybody seen my mouse?

Bedtime is story time on Coe Road
and in Bob's hands
the occasion for imagination,
participation, fun.

The Camel Who Took a Walk
brings out a Woodruff chorus of
"La la la lump, da lump, da lump!
La la la lump, da lump, da lump!"

Rain at bedtime?
John had
Great Big
Waterproof
Boots on . . .

Now, washing hands against the pandemic,
grateful for my health and our family, I hear,
. . . Emmeline!
Where have you been?

Where have you been?
Why, it's not more than a week!" And Emmeline
Said, "Sillies, I went and saw the Queen.
She says my hands are purfickly clean!"

Three butts in the air,
three voices, one deep, cry plaintively,
Has anybody seen my mouse?

(with gratitude to A. A. Milne for *When We Were Very Young*, 1924, and Jack Tworkov, for *The Camel Who Took a Walk*, 1967)

Waking

In the early dawn I turn to you,
press my body the length of yours,
curl my arm around your waist,
feel the familiar ins and outs
of this body I know so well.

Lying here, I draw strength
and comfort from your being.
I ground myself
in your steadfastness,
your optimism and encouragement.

How is it, then,
in the midst of all these riches
I lie here
feeling such sadness,
such longing?

Return

I am uneasy as I turn the corner into our street.
After ten days of woman space, talk, retreat, writing,
I feel I am turned inside out.
Where is my skin? The protective coat is missing,
Grief, a deep well of pain,
has mottled my chest and throat,
swollen my eyes for days, miles.
How will *you* be?

We share our feelings—
your exhaustion, my anxiety.
We talk nonstop through unpacking,
showering, dinner at La Fiesta,
mail and messages, going to bed;
we tell stories, laugh, commiserate.
It is easy, comfortable,
to hear each other's news,
tell someone who can hear
and laugh, know.
We are light.

You sleep deeply.
I waken in the night, stunned
at the thought of not waking with you.
There is so much I've learned,
so much I want to tell you—
How will *you* be?

You waken, we touch gently,
smile softly. It's there in our eyes,
a tentative hope still flickering—
even breathing these words
may put it out, so I am cautious.
How will *you* be?

There is so much to say—
You are my familiar,
I breathe to myself,
adding, *yes.*

What's Wrong?

What's wrong? he asks,
You're so quiet.

Nothing, I reply.

How I wish he knew the magic
of quiet, wanted
to plumb the depths,
drift slowly in languid currents,
pierce darkness with light,
explore for treasure.

How I'd love
to see him emerge, eyes shining,
excitedly turning a find
this way and that in his hands, breathless,
pointing to the pearl he found
there in the silent
deep.

What's wrong? he asks,
You're so quiet.

Nothing, I reply, thinking,
Everything.

The Explorer and the Writer

An explorer and a writer sat at the kitchen table
speaking their dreams.

I want the world, said the explorer,
his eyes sparkling with enthusiasm,
I want to see everything
taste everything
have everything.
This is my time, an exciting time,
my bags are packed, I'm ready;
come with me.

The writer felt exhausted.

I want solitude, said the writer,
her eyes fired with determination,
I want to know everything
feel everything
understand everything.
I'm on a journey to my soul, an interior time,
I need solace and peace while I work
to come home.

The explorer felt confused.

An explorer and a writer sat at the kitchen table
speaking their dreams;
the north and the south winds
blowing together
at the door.

Pantoum for a Marriage

I'm not ready to let go of this marriage.
We were friends before we were lovers,
we support each other, are good to each other
thirty-three years, five homes, two grown children, thousands of memories.

We were friends before we were lovers,
laughter, talking and faith sustain us
thirty-three years, five homes, two grown children, thousands of memories:
the joyous, painful stuff of life.

Laughter, talking and faith sustain us;
through deaths of first-born son, parents and illusions,
the joyous, painful stuff of life,
we create safe harbor.

Through deaths of first-born son, parents and illusions
we hang in, solid, through thick and thin,
we create safe harbor,
people feel whole around us, they say.

We hang in, solid, through thick and thin,
we love what we are when together in public;
people feel whole around us, they say,
but loneliness rises like steam when the doors close.

We love what we are when together in public.
In private we grow cautious, polite with each other,
and loneliness rises like steam when the doors close;
we give our best to others.

In private we grow cautious, polite with each other,
the anger erupts violently, we are frightened;
we give our best to others
and lie awake at three in the morning.

The anger erupts violently, we are frightened;
we wonder if we will make it for the second half
and lie awake at three in the morning
praying for wisdom.

We wonder if we will make it for the second half,
we support each other, are good to each other;
praying for wisdom
I'm not ready to let go of this marriage.

Tybee Island, Georgia, February

Gray sky, windblown beach,
surf crashes recklessly,
foam whips sideways,
is swallowed in undertow
before its fragrance can be delivered.
Gusts drive sand shrapnel into our legs,
sea gulls stand about in rows squinting,
arch their shoulders against the cold;
ungainly pelicans pull themselves
along the shore
struggling upwind.

We pace the beach to the inlet buoy
leaning into the wind.
You, collar turned up,
walk straight ahead,
your eyes cool gray-green,
not the warm hazel ones I've known.
A stranger mouths your words,
dry tight syllables that raise welts,
another stranger answers in my voice—
disbelief, pleading—

I do not speak of my own betrayal.
That I too have found a woman to love
is terror and typhoon of its own;
I had hoped to sort this out in safety.
All this you know and do not know.

Broken promises swirl at our feet.
We come to the end, turn,
are tossed like a couple of sanderlings
back to our start in silence.
Foam follows and
gritty sand stings our feet
as we return to the car.

Change of Seasons

Trees blaze
against a pewter sky
burnished in Flemish light,
hurl color against my eyes
which sting with aching.
These leaves will fall,
leave trunks and branches,
now scarcely noticeable,
stripped naked against the cold,
each tree reduced
to its winter essence,
growing unseen buds.

And you, my love, and us—
we catch in my throat,
reflect in pictures everywhere,
smiling, golden in goodness,
so brilliant in this final display
I actually long
for winter's wind
to rip the leaves from my branches,
rake this perfection out of sight,
blow it behind me.
Then I too can stand stark,
roots deep,
tapped into my own
winter essence,
listening for spring.

Grace Notes

We met celebrating ourselves as fifty-somethings,
        a day for reflection,
                renewal;
                        we connected through sharing,
                              creativity and, finally,
                                    compassion.
I held her while she cried,
        a simple act;
                something behind her eyes
                        said I might offer,
                              something behind my heart
                                  said I wanted to.
Soon we met again
        over poetry and photography,
                Dutch babies and flower-garnished grapefruit,
                        over spirituality, sexuality,
                              laughter, sudden tears—
                                  over and over.
We fell into each other
        as naturally
                as water falls over a ledge
                        inevitably, joyously, musically
                              tumbling toward the froth
                                  and the clear pool below.
Walking my forest and her lake paths,
        we danced our lives for each other,
                told our hopes, our terrors,
                        sang our souls' journeys,
                              slaked each other's thirst
                                  for listening.

Gently she led me into her world,
      unwrapped mysteries,
            shined light on another
               way of being,
                    slowly drew, never pulled
                         me to that knowing.
I followed willingly,
      wanting to wrap myself
        in her,
            wanting to know myself
              this way,
                  know her.

Yet I retreated, hesitating;
      I placed restraints on us and
        still she held space
            with patient heart and open palms
              which I experienced
                  as incredible grace.

If My Hands Could Speak

If my hands could speak
they would remember murmuring
how her hair might feel,
remember the prickling of my palms
in her presence,
an unbreathable blush
spreading over my body.

If my hands could speak
they would remember whispering
would her hair feel soft or stiff
if I combed her curls
with my outstretched fingers.
My hands would recall being clenched,
steepled in prayer.

If my hands could speak
they would shout with joy
the memory they hold
of that day when longing
reached across the chasm between us,
pulled her over
and touched her hair.

Departure

Her eyes go first.
They go from green to gray,
examine dust particles
in sunbeams,
cast about for black holes,
anything but me.

And then her jaw,
tense, as if she trudges
across a desolate tundra,
head down against oncoming sleet,
dragging her belongings alone
to some Siberian outpost.

I know this brutal journey began
on the lap of a predator priest,
one lone bulb casting shadows
on a lunchroom wall,
the projector stuttering
a black and white comedy.

Her melancholy lingers
after she's gone. An Arctic wind
chills the gulf between us.
I shiver, hunch my shoulders,
wait, harnessing my anger,
for her return.

Pantoum for a Love

This is not what you wanted to hear
I'll say it as gently as possible
I'm not ready to let go of this marriage
A tapestry of memory, promises, plans.

I'll say it as gently as possible
I need to move slowly
A tapestry of memory, promises, plans—
I'm awash in my feelings.

I need to move slowly
Your eyes fall into my soul
I'm awash in my feelings
My fingers reach for you when you're not here.

Your eyes fall into my soul
Our bodies sing fire
My fingers reach for you when you're not here
The yearning is an ocean that rises and falls in me.

Our bodies sing fire
Meeting beyond imagination
The yearning is an ocean that rises and falls in me
And so is my grief.

Meeting beyond imagination
The future is out of focus
And so is my grief
I retreat in solitude to fathom myself.

The future is out of focus
The present plays bittersweet tunes on an antique instrument
I retreat in solitude to fathom myself
Time to pluck the threads and honor them.

The present plays bittersweet tunes on an antique instrument
I'm not ready to let go of this marriage
Time to pluck the threads and honor them
This is not what you wanted to hear.

Your Green Eyes

I would have loved you sooner if I hadn't been afraid,
for instantly I knew that I was met;
your green eyes smiled, moved in, unpacked and stayed.

Our stories kindled, then when words would fade,
my inner terror doused the flames in sweat.
I would have loved you sooner if I hadn't been afraid.

My life was ordered, all the plans were laid—
that Whidbey beach house filled with family—yet
your green eyes smiled, moved in, unpacked and stayed.

You challenged me, I felt myself evade
while trying close and closer still to get.
I would have loved you sooner if I hadn't been afraid.

I wondered how your hair would feel; I prayed
my hands that notion and all others would forget;
your green eyes smiled, moved in, unpacked and stayed.

Now, though we walk in fire, I wouldn't trade
this sense of home with you for any on a bet.
I would have loved you sooner if I hadn't been afraid;
your green eyes smiled, moved in, unpacked and stayed.

Low Tide

I, ocean,
distance myself again and again,
surge in the middle of nowhere
a raging boil of emotion
spit foam and fury from the tips of my swells
—I'm deep, so proudly deep—
beware the deadly behemoths
rampaging beneath my surface.

You, beach,
anchored to the shore
lie open and without guile
your secrets exposed
to eyes and feet that probe your sandbars,
you shelter life in the shallows
nourish razor clams, great blue heron, Bonaparte gulls,
and patiently wait, gathering warmth,

for my inevitable
return.

You Loved Me Bigger

You loved me bigger than I expected to be loved.
Again and again you spread your palms,
blew me loose with your sweet breath,
smiled me floating into the freedom
of myself.

You loved me bigger than I knew how to say.
Before your wisdom I was silent—
a child, a student
in awe of your selfless teaching,
your generous love.

You loved me bigger than I imagined to be loved.
You listened to my struggle and responded with
understanding, tenderly repackaging my words
so I heard myself making more sense
than I thought I could.

You loved me bigger
until I knew how to be.

Hold, Release

Like silver spoons and pull aparts
a circle yin and yang entwined,
we hold release, these kindred hearts.

At first we hung on every kind
of nuance, story, turn of mind
like silver spoons, not pull aparts.

But then, maturing, not to bind,
discovered strength when we're inclined
to hold release, these kindred hearts.

Together joy, delight we find
yet space is crucial. We unwind
like silver spoons to pull aparts.

Zestful love's a fruit with rind
whose very boundaries are designed
to hold, release, these kindred hearts.

My blood still races with my mind
when we are close, yet I'm resigned
to hold, release, these kindred hearts,
silver spoons and pull aparts.

Wonder

Does a tree trunk thank the leaves
shading its roots for the miracle
of photosynthesis that gives it life?
Does the horizon thank the sky
for painting benediction each evening,
streaking its hills with crimson gold?

Does a footpath thank the feet
whose determined passing keeps it open?
Do flat stones thank the children
who skip them on the lake's rim?
Do those stones shout
joy at unexpected lightness?

Does breath thank laughter
for shaking it loose from a ribbed prison?
Does a honeycomb thank the bees who fill it?
Does the heart, in the dark where no one hears,
whisper *thank you* to soul
for the song it sings?

Does beach thank ocean when, after a pounding storm,
it runs its fingers gently up her back
easing the knots and ripples raised by wind,
draws her gently down to the edge where,
in the foam and running sanderlings,
they rest together, ebb and flow?

I wonder,
that of all the possibilities in life,
you and I found our ways to each other,
that here we stand able to name
our binding—heart, soul, body—married.
A toast! To state, to family, to friends, to love.
A toast! To wonder.

(for Mary, February 10, 2013, our wedding day)

FAITH, FEAR, and FURY

I've always been in love with the church. I was lucky to marry a man who was also a life-long Presbyterian and who loved and served the church as I did. Church provided friends, stoked our faith, inspired the best in us, gave us opportunities to give and grow—even launched me on my career.

Church also is the place where my very *being* has been challenged the most, given the events and timing of my life and my determination to wrestle with them.

This section points to the centrality of faith—and church—in all my life.

Early Voice

You can choose not to hear,
not to be;
there are plenty of things to do
while denying—
work, serve, run, hide—
and many will be good for the world,
bring you credit, do no harm.

Yet there comes a time to answer,
when the voice will be stilled no longer,
when in the darkness of your own soul
you must stop—
turn, sit, face this call—
say yes I will,
or no, I cannot, will not.

God will love you
no matter your choice,
will hold you in compassion,
understand your fear—
neither shame nor deplore—
will even comfort you
if terror has you in a vice.

God will also stand with you
if you say yes,
go forth with you as you live this voice
which may be God's spirit—
knit into you from the beginning—
wishing only that you will bring your self
wholly to the world.

Turn Over the Tables

The church, it seems,
is on the block,
        going
                going
                        gone—
sold to the highest bidders,
those with the most money,
simplicity of absolutes,
utter confidence
that their authority
comes straight
from God Almighty Himself.

God Almighty!

Jesus—
do you weep
to see your body
broken again
        for a few
                pieces of
                        silver?

(Written on the resignation under pressure of Mary Ann Lundy from her position as head of Church-Wide Planning for the Presbyterian Church (USA) because she played a leadership role in the 1993 interfaith event, "Re-Imagining: a Global Theological Conference by Women." Presbyterians offended by some parts of the Re-Imagining conference threatened to withhold their donations to the PC(USA), leading to Lundy's termination.)

For Jane Adams Spahr

Go ahead, Janie,
you've earned it—
get up there in the pulpit
and preach to us.
Help us to polish our piety,
our Pharasitic worship of the rules,
give us something to sneer at
from our sanctimonious safety in these pews—

or

Perhaps you will speak to us
with the voice of the Galilean,
look through our sin with loving eyes,
call us to greatness and partnership
in spite of our willingness to persecute you,
to deny your part in us,
to let you take the rap for our own cowardice.
Go ahead, Janie, preach,
please.

(Written in protest of the Presbyterian Church (U.S.A.) General Assembly Permanent Judicial Commission's decision to overturn the ordination of the Rev. Jane Spahr because she was a lesbian in relationship with a woman.)

Holy Week

1.

It doesn't seem possible—
one minute I was riding on a borrowed ass,
the crowds screaming *Hosanna!*
children waving palm fronds,
grown men spreading their cloaks
to soften my path—
and now I kneel here, alone,
even my friends unable to keep
vigil with me.

Alone, I face my own death,
more searing than any
I would choose.
Can I bear the pain?
I doubt. I fear.
God, my God, where are you?
Hear me, won't you?
I want out!
Please.

2.

I don't know,
he looks OK to me;
besides, the light in his eyes
goes straight to my soul;
I want him to see goodness
in me to match his own.
I cannot condemn him.
Basin, please.

3.
I don't know him,
not if it's going to cost me,
not if I might be arrested too,
shamed, humiliated,
held up to public scorn,
risk trial, even death—
not I,
I don't know him.

4.
My son, my dear son,
now you've done it.
Couldn't we have had
a few more years? You're
much too young. I'm
not ready. Why?
Why now?

5.
Thank you,
thank you for the water
I draw from the cloth you proffer,
thank you for catching me
as I stumbled back there,
thank you for the kindness
I read in your silently respectful eyes
as I carry my shame
through your midst.

6.
His body
broken for me,
his blood shed
for me,
the lamb of God
walks to the slaughter
carrying his own mortality.

7.
This year will be different.
I have my own Golgotha,
my own Peter who denies me,
my own Pilate who just wants peace
undisturbed by a Galilean
who sees into my soul
with acceptance and love.
I have my own crowd in me
who can cheer or detract
with equal vehemence,
my own mother who just wanted me
to be ordinary
and live a long life in the village.
What I need to find
in the darkness of my own tomb
is the living water, truth and grace,
if this year is to be different.

Tomb Time

Life and death at once,
wave after wave of grief overtakes,
groans in someone else's voice
leaves a gulping emptiness, spent
in a borrowed spot, no permanent
resting place: tomb time.

Some of us run from the tomb;
disappointment and disillusion win over faith.
We who wanted to be on the winning team
disappear when it looks like our side lost;
doubt and uncertainty drive us away
from tomb time.

Some of us, knowing our own unfaithfulness,
the treachery with which we engineered
this tomb time,
slink away in shame,
not sure we can live or that we deserve to.
All of us are scared in tomb time.

What alchemy was with the crucified
we know not; we speculate
he confronted dark spirits,
did business in unseen, unspeakable waters,
coming somehow to terms with them.
All we know is that goodness was gone in tomb time.

For now, it is my own tomb time,
choices and consequences clash,
dark spirits and darker thoughts,
roll over me like that stone of old,
suffocate with grief's metallic taste
all goodness lost in the dank of tomb time.

Easter Sunrise, 1994

Once more we tug on warm
clothes and boots, carry chairs
through predawn gray
to a bare cross on the church lawn,
sit in silence hearing the birds
declare the glory of God,
feel rather than actually see
the lightening of the day,
our thin morning voices a fine mist
rising over the traffic behind us:
Jesus Christ is risen today!
Lifted by the words,
Christ is risen! He is risen indeed!

What is risen in me this Eastertide?
Honesty? Or at least a willingness
to roll the stone away from the tomb
of silence? Does a white-clad angel
sit inside to greet those who come
looking for you, reassure us
we have nothing to fear?
Is it Honesty, Lord?

What is risen in me this Eastertide?
Surrender? *Let this cup pass from me,*
I prayed, hardly daring to continue
nonetheless, not my will but yours be done.
Is this your will, Lord?
Here am I, Lord. You made me.
Can I do it, simply be me?
Is it Surrender, Lord?

What is risen in me this Eastertide?
Courage, Lord? Can I call myself
out of this tomb of terror
into the light of your love and leading,
offer myself to whatever service
you may have in store for me,
can I trust that much?
Is it Courage, Lord?

Let all things seen and unseen
Their notes in gladness blend,
For Christ the Lord has risen,
Our joy that hath no end.
The closing Hymn wafts over the gathering.
We rise, fold chairs, smile at friends,
already tasting cheesy egg casserole,
head back to our cars, warm now.
Oh Lord, yes, I pray, may
Honesty, Surrender, and Courage
rise in me this Eastertide.

Say Nothing

What to say about the church?
Say it betrays me.
Say the Pharisees are winning the battle,
say narrowness and fear have taken captive
the followers of the Lord of Love.
Say the church has lost its heart,
say its moral beacon pierces with cold white light,
makes life a harsh and colorless choice
between glare and shadow.
Say the church is a family
squabbling over power and control,
say the elder brothers refuse
to attend the party
if the prodigals are coming.

What to say about God?
Say God is still in charge
and—patiently or vengefully—
will win this war.

What to say about my rage?
Say nothing.

(In early 1997, I was a delegate to the Seattle Presbytery when an amendment to The Book of Order, the Presbyterian Church (USA)'s constitution, was defeated. The amendment would have allowed the ordination of gay deacons, elders and pastors. I, an ordained elder for twenty years, though at that time very much in the closet, voted FOR the amendment. The above was my response.)

Tsunami of Grief

The church that I love is rejecting me
for my love and my being by some I am banned—
tsunami of grief on a turbulent sea.

For years as an elder I counseled and planned
but now there's no Session on which I could stand—
the church that I love is rejecting me.

Clerics immaculate, collared and tanned
obliterate childhood with wayward hands—
tsunami of grief on a turbulent sea.

Conservative narrowness outward has fanned
with speeches and judgments so tidily canned
the church that I love is rejecting me.

I wonder what Jesus would write in the sand
if he walked and observed all about in this land
tsunami of grief on a turbulent sea.

I suspect that his words would be avidly panned
by Pharisees by whom his body is manned
as the church that I love is rejecting me—
tsunami of grief on a turbulent sea.

(In January of 2001, the Seattle Presbytery met to vote again on an amendment
which would change *The Book of Order* to allow churches to ordain deacons,
elders or pastors who are gay. I was asked to be one of the official speakers FOR
the Amendment when it came to the floor for a Presbytery vote. I had served our
Presbytery in several capacities. I hoped my credibility might carry some weight,
even as it meant I would publically "out" myself to the larger church. Heart in
mouth, I spoke. The Presbytery soundly rejected the amendment. I was absolutely
crushed. The after-effects lasted for months. It was half a year later before I could
give words to my disheartenment.)

Release, 2020

I hold my church in open palms,
no longer clutching the reins.

It will be a joy to let church
wash over me like water
I can welcome or let flow away,
no need to direct, explain, defend.

May I be as gentle with myself
and others as I intend to be
with my church.

Beach Haiku, June 22, 2020

Shell broken open
by COVID, racism, church,
fresh air fills spaces.

This stone—strong, white, flawed—
warm in my hand from sunshine
reminds me of me.

Tiny limpet shell
shining among rocks and grit
open to what's next.

She Wraps the House Around Her

She wraps the house around her.
Arriving at the top of the lane,
she stills her engine,
unlocks the door, and
sinks into sunlight,
flowers, fireplace,
music.

She wraps the house around her,
sits in the crook of its arm,
smells pungent grasses, watches trees burst,
waits for the eagle she once saw
circling overhead to return,
listens to the buzz of insects,
beat of her own heart.

She wraps the house around her.
Solitude like she has never known
is her companion now.
At night she dims the lights,
settles into the couch, her eyes
on lights across the lake;
she is rising from a dark place.

She wraps the house around her,
cooks a feast for friends
who midwifed her,
celebrating, with champagne
and laughter,
the miracle
of rebirth.

WOMEN IN BLACK

Women in Black is an international movement begun in 1988 when Israeli Jewish and Palestinian mothers, dressed in black, stood together in a public silent vigil, calling for an end to, as they said, "My son seeking to kill your son, and your son seeking to kill mine." The movement spread to Northern Ireland, where Catholic and Protestant mothers stood together, holding the same yearning.

Bellevue's *Women in Black* have been standing vigil for peace on the corner of Bellevue Way and NE 8th Street from noon to 1 p.m. every Saturday since the run up to the Gulf War in 1991. I stood with them for nearly twenty years, beginning when I was beside myself with anger that our nation would start war just because we had the might to do so. Our local members have stood with *Women in Black* in Paris, London, and many other places in the world.

I no longer stand with *Women in Black*. To be honest, I despaired that our work was making any difference, as wars continue, tearing up the Middle East and shredding so many of our soldiers' lives when they return from duty. The friends I stood with still stand, every Saturday, without fail. I dedicate this section as a tribute to them.

These poems were inspired by our standing together.

There's a Poem in Here

There's a poem in here, but I cannot find it. My week old granddaughter, when she's awake, regards the world with a somber, reflective expression. I hold her and watch in wonder as she explores her surroundings. What does she see in the movement of light and shadow? What does she make of this world so much roomier and brighter than the one she inhabited just days ago? Before she drifts off to sleep again, she gives a lazy, laughing smile of recognition, pleasure flooding her features. I wonder if she is communicating with angels who are watching her in the room, telling them she made a good choice. As for me, I hold this miracle to my heart, fierce in my conviction to fight against the gathering darkness, the great not-to-be-spoken-within-these-walls menace of my own country's leaders and others who plan mutual destruction. Outside the sun is shining, and further outside soldiers are packing their fatigues and weapons, boarding troop ships and fighter jets, other leaders are sitting in tense circles listening to one another, testing, testing. Suspicion and inevitability threaten to eclipse the very sun that attracts these tiny eyes I am coming to love beyond words, and the knowledge of my own inability to protect her takes my breath away. There's a poem in here, but I cannot find it. Yet.

Fire with Fire

What do you do
with a terrorist?
How do you contain a man like Saddam
who boils people in acid,
encourages torture, rape, murder,
has the capability for gas and germ warfare,
the determination to dominate his world,
the power to bring oil-dependent nations
to their knees?

Was there no other way
than to slaughter so many of his people,
devastate an ancient city?
Did that even reach him,
he who has no observable regard for humankind?

Now that we have joined him
in a duel of power and destruction,
how can we maintain a claim on our national virtue?

   We can't.

Now,
we have proved we are as cold-blooded as he.
We have thoroughly demonstrated our own dark side,
exposed our own capacity for terrorism,
and dishonored our nation's dignity.

Video Games

War-making.
We're good at it.
We do it so professionally,
We don't even feel the pain—
        the enemy's or ours.

We rain fire on Baghdad, leave it in ruins.
With pinpoint accuracy,
we blow up tanks in the desert.
We pick off convoys and then fly
back to our bases with broad smiles, thumbs-up,
to attend celebratory pep rallies.

Our view of the savagery of this Iraq war
is one bear of a Schwarzkopf in Army fatigues
and distant explosions
brought to our homes
through the evening news.

Our president declares, "Mission Accomplished!"
We rejoice that we've lost so few people;
we pray with relief that it's over,
that nearly all of our young men and women
will be coming home.
We thank God for blessing America.

Is God pleased,
does God bless the fact
that our military is so high-tech,
that we excel at such detached destruction
we may as well be playing
video games?

When I See Only Us and Them

When I see only us and them,
when I look at you and see other,
when your otherness unsettles me,
I can start war.

When I see you as other,
I can be as dangerous
as any enemy you can imagine,
as capable of violence.

When I thank God I am not you,
I wrap my self-righteous cloak close,
smug in my superiority.
Watch out—I may start war.

Sisterhood

I love my children.
I desire nothing more than
that they grow up
in robust health, undamaged
by hatred and suspicion,
safe from hunger, disease, and war;
that they learn compassion,
nurture the next generation
and their community
toward wholeness.

I live in a country
where I can hold such dreams.
Not everyone does.

How do you love your children,
you sister mother in your hijab
peering out from a war-shattered home,
young children clinging to your abaya
half a world—and more—
from me?

What you desire for your children
I cannot know. Still
I hold my desires,
dream such things.
I want them for your children too.

If only we might stand vigil together
on a street corner, Iraqi Muslim woman
and American Christian, holding high
our hopes for our children and
our conviction that war between them
has no place in our dreams!

Thank You For Your Service

Inspired by a news analysis by Matt Richtel,
"Please Don't Thank Me for My Service."
(*New York Times*, February 21, 2015)

"Thank you for your service, son," we say,
heaping praise on any vet we meet,
not noticing he looks the other way.

Pausing briefly in our busy day,
our words a mantra we repeat:
"Thank you for your service, son," we say.

We know it's tough out there, amidst the fray,
defending us through sandstorm, mud, and heat—
we hardly note he looks the other way.

We're proud of you—and glad we haven't paid,
nor sent our loved ones, risked their lives so sweet—
yet, "Thank you for your service, son," we say.

Our flag unfurled, we hold our guilt at bay
and breathe a sigh as he walks down the street,
not noticing he looks the other way.

We have no ante in this pot to pay,
perhaps no right to even touch his feet,
still, "Thank you for your service, son," we say,
not noticing he looks the other way.

Prisoners of War

A passer-by reminds us:

> *Famous scene in the movie M.A.S.H.:*
> *Two doctors working on patients in the O.R.*
> *One says to the other,*
>> *"Why are you working so hard to save him?*
>> *He's a prisoner of war."*
> *The other surgeon says to his buddy,*
>> *"So are you."*

Aren't we all prisoners of war?

War captures our treasure, keeps it hostage.
Young men and women
> return from this captivity changed forever,
> their eyes reviewing horrors we can't imagine,
> dreams forever disrupted.
Bridges collapse, we lack the funds to repair them,
  we're busy destroying bridges elsewhere.
Teachers struggle,
> buy—if they can—their own supplies.
The poor become poorer,
> there is less and less help for them.
Our attention is diverted.

Could we break out of this prison of endless war,
we might focus on saving our planet,
repairing our own country's brokenness,
lifting up those who are wounded.
We might feed the hungry,
care for the children,
live toward justice for all.

May we do it!
May we break the bonds of warfare,
begin to redream this fractured world,
salvage all of creation
and live lives worthy of humanity.

"Why are you working so hard to save him?
He's a prisoner of war."
"So are you."

So are we all.

LOVE SONGS

I think of these poems as tributes— to people, to moments
worth celebrating, and to the sheer joy I've had writing poetry.

Church

Month after month,
year after year,
it's a sacred vow
to gather, the third or, now
the second Monday.

They arrive with joy,
greet each other,
breathe gratitude and relief,
settle into whatever pew
is available.

Soon the hymns begin,
stirring anthems, hosannas,
canticles of memory,
psalms and praises,
a laud of life.

Confession and absolution
shine in the honesty
among them. There is nothing
they cannot hear,
they haven't heard.

Prayers too, petitions
for children, grandchildren,
spouses, our wounded world, oh, Lord—
be with them, help us,
show us the way.

It goes without saying
there is always communion.
Elements raised—bread passed,
wine poured. The gifts of God
for the people of God.

Offering too. They do not skimp
on their promises to be faithful,
to listen attentively, to give what they can,
to walk each other home,
when the time comes.

And oh, God, is there ever thanksgiving!
They never leave without the hallelujah
of gratitude. That they are here
together. That they have another day
ahead for worship together.

Finally, it's a benediction of blessing
to know that while they are separate,
their prayers soar to the skies and lift them,
wherever and whenever they ask—
and even if they don't.

Now that—
that is church.
Real church.
And the sisters said—
AMEN!

*(The sisters who say AMEN! are a group of eight friends who've know each
other for more than forty-five years. We came together as a Bible study/prayer/
share group, and stuck as friends. We still meet once a month year-round
without fail—and as often as we can or as is necessary in between.)*

Why I Prefer Thanksgiving to Christmas

A circle of extended family
bound by history,
generations knit by choice
and reunited by choice,
we stand, hold hands,
smiling around the ring.

We've been through life
together, shared heartaches
enough to leave us breathless.
We've partied to late hours,
hiked over mountains,
camped in deluges,
run racing rivers,
then showed up to serve
the church together.

This circle, this prayer, reconnects
us with what matters most,
why we are here—
gratitude for this family,
for those no longer standing here,
for our children and grandchildren
and that they seem poised
to carry on together.

No gifts, received or given,
no dancing light displays,
no flaming figgy pudding,
no joyous Christmas Eve
comes near the Hallelujah Chorus
right here—all of us again
shining in this circle,
radiant with Thanksgiving.

(We found each other at church in 1973, six couples new to the Pacific Northwest and most without extended family near. We say we picked each other to be aunties and uncles to our children. We've celebrated Thanksgiving weekends together, often at Fort Worden State Park in Port Townsend, WA, for more than forty years.)

L' Chaim!

Maybe this is as good as it gets:
on a crisp late summer night
when we could have been
at another memorial service
or sitting in a movie,
we—circle of friends become family—
gather around a smoky bonfire, throw
pinecones and celebration into the flames.

We are linked through mystery
of illness and life,
miraculously aware—
yes, we know it!—
that at this moment
of reprieve for our friend Marian,
nothing else matters more
than being here, being together.

That we will die
hangs there in the shadows,
we all know it, feel
its breath on our necks.
Still, tonight,
we turn our backs on it,
draw closer together
face the fire, glow with grace.

Big Hearts

You know it as soon as the door opens—
big hearts live here.
They embrace—with full-body hugs—
all who enter.
They expect you'll bring laughter with you—
and if you're short on it, they've got laughter to share
and intend to do it.
They expect you to fit right in—
and before you know it, you do.
If you come bearing a story, happy or despairing, they listen—
with joy, compassion, without judgment.

These big hearts keep people close.
They are part of a tribe of long-time friends and their families,
know each other's histories, vacation together,
gather frequently in clusters for big or small reasons—
and if you're in town, you are instantly a member
of the tribe, and they don't forget you.

Oh, and yes, these big hearts have names—
Nicolle, a mom and teacher as generous and sensitive as her Aunty Mary;
Gerald, a father with fun and *what's next?* up his sleeve;
Alli, expressive, expansive, who'll try anything, and usually succeeds;
Logan, easy-going, gentle, a gaming whiz with a wicked sense of humor;
Opa, a Bavarian grandpa with a ready smile and a twinkle in his eye
even now that Oma's gone;
Ricki, a grandma whose steady presence warms the house out front;
Sylv, Pat, Hannah and Gracie, Gerald's sister and family, just blocks away.

Big hearts all—
generous, joyous, with love to spare—
you know it as soon as the door opens.

"You Belong to Me"

(Jo Stafford song)

It's the early 50's; we sway side to side
humming into each other's ears:
" . . . *pyramids along the Nile . . .*
just remember darling all the while,
you belong to me."

Not for us matching ski sweaters,
the high school fad that proclaims
"You Belong to Me." Still
we rock slowly, ever so slowly
pressing our dreams into each other.

Oh, how little we knew then!
We never dreamed your West Point brother
would run a car through someone,
ruin his marriage with alcohol or
that you'd become his keeper.

Never suspected that years later
I would leave my husband—
the man whose Colgate fraternity
you wouldn't pledge—
and join my life happily to a woman.

We held on to each other most of our teens,
made our parents nervous about more
than just our different religions,
hummed "You Belong to Me"
as though it meant forever.

Now we settle into wing chairs in the hall,
with another glass of wine,
nod good night to quizzical glances
from old friends on their way home
and catch up after our 55th reunion dinner.

We have much to say, as old friends.
Funny, isn't it,
that even now,
in a singular way,
"you belong to me."

Sight

Did I tell you about the girl I met in Scheveningen?
My father's eyes would light up
as he retold the tale: his midshipman cruise,
shore leave, the Dutch lass who later wrote him
a note he kept for years in a trunk
beside his Naval Academy dress uniform.

My father had a way with women.
He tamed my mother—no mean feat, as she was tinder
ready to ignite most of her life.
The preacher's kid in him held the line
between courtliness and teasing, yet it was always clear
he appreciated women, and they him.

By the time his namesake, my son,
graduated from college, macular degeneration
had staked a claim on my father's eyesight.
Still, he worked harder that anyone I ever knew
to see—*Oh, that tree over there!*
How's that for a golden color!

When I missed him at Jim's graduation party
in the Alumni House, I found my father on a chair
in the hall. *Are you OK,* I asked?
Oh yes, he beamed, gesturing up to a window on the landing.
I'm watching the sun shine through the girls' dresses
as they come down the stairs. See the legs!

Mirrors

My mother was a windstorm whipping dust across the plains of childhood
sudden rampages shrouded the considerable good in her and left us
disoriented
on laundry days she stomped up the basement steps to the back yard
stabbed clothespins into place huffing indignation into the air

In the kitchen she fretted over the yeast rising fat splattering chicken parts
heaved exasperated sighs hissed her dissatisfaction into the houseplants
rehearsed arguments with people who needed to be straightened out
I just detest Mamie Eisenhower she exploded one day, *sotto voce.*

Who knew the source of these furies?
Rage barely contained her pursed lips spit wrath just below the surface
once in a while she would startle look quickly around to see
who else was listening   we all were

Her fuming was the barometer we checked to see if a day would be fair or
foul
mercury could drop in an instant foreshadowing turbulence
we became watchful honed our skills at hunkering
swore we would never

Now I look in the mirror to see my mother, catch my own voice
whispering conversations I will never have with people I don't know, and
more,
sometimes when I heave my own sigh and don't notice, hear my daughter
laugh
you're getting it, mom, you're getting it.

Homebodies

Ruth and Jim Sparklin were partners
in nearly everything they did.

The only school nights they ever left home
they went to Rochester's Home Bureau.
They took classes there that enhanced our home.
They stenciled Hitchcock chairs together,
antiqued the old upright piano;
my father caned the dining room chairs,
my mother etched intricate lamp shades.
When Daddy took up decoupage,
he decorated wooden tops of straw purses
for every woman in the family, and Mother
lined each one with personally chosen fabric.

They made icicle pickles together every year.
This took weeks, both of them pouring out,
boiling and repouring the brine into the ceramic
crock until the pickles were perfect.
My sister and I called them *ickle pickles*,
and the name stuck. We always had enough
for the whole year; they were always delicious.

I grew up knowing that a blessing
of my childhood was our dinner table,
where we stayed until the coffee pot
was empty; where Mother read letters
from relatives; when the day's events,
including my father's work
and our play or school, were digested.

That another one was the sound of
their conversation drifting upstairs
to my bedroom every night,
music that put me to sleep.

Now, looking back,
I see that one I missed
was how their enjoyment
of each other
kept us secure.

Tangibles

and why am I only now writing about these many creations?

> I see her at the dining room table.
> It is strewn with fabric, Singer at the ready.
> She made nearly all our clothes, even
> tailoring a pink coat and bonnet for me
> one Easter. My father took a picture
> of me in it; the story goes I had just said,
> "I can beat up any kid in my class but
> Hermie Judd," as he snapped it.
> She had our sizes down, even as we grew.
> When I was in college she mailed me
> a cherry *peau de soie* cocktail dress
> I could put right on and wear to
> Winter Party at Colgate.

and how could I forget her knitting?

> Mittens and sweaters—the more complicated,
> the better: fisherman's knit, Fair Isle patterns,
> she made them for all of us, even matching
> red pullovers for Katie and me when Katie
> was a toddler—and she forgave me for
> shrinking Katie's in the dryer.
> She made granny square afghans for each of
> four granddaughters when they went to college,
> so complex my father had to figure out the
> patterns, each in a different color scheme,
> no two squares alike.
> Jim kept his afghan, a deep blue, for years.
> Mine, soft cream, warms me still on cold nights.

and why am I only now acknowledging this
> tangible evidence of my mother's lasting devotion?

Music

(for Katie)

You hold an infant long before you see her.

She sings in your heart when you first suspect
        she may be on the way.

You speak to her as she flutters in your womb.
        You dream of her and
        for her as you embrace
        your expanding belly, feel your own beating heart.

You marvel as she stretches and turns,
        a miracle, dancing in the dark,
        getting ready for her debut.

By the time she is in your arms
        you have already loved her beyond words,
        and what you hold now
            is music.

Tea Leaves—January 27, 2003

It was one of those moments.
I lay on the sofa in a Chicago suburb
with my new baby girl, hearing
my mother pour boiling water into a teapot.
She arranged ginger cookies on a glass plate,
carried all this fragrance to the living room,
smiled shyly at me as she poured two cups.
"It must feel like a short time," I said,
imagining her mother pouring tea for her
when I was new. "Yes," said my mother,
a memory rearranging her face,
"It goes fast."

Twenty-some years later
I made tea for that same baby girl, now resolute,
brought it to her on the sofa where she lay
cramping. It had been a short
drive over the Berkeley hills,
a brief magazine read in the waiting room
before we collected her, pale and determined,
for the quiet ride home. The next day,
she and I went to a nursery and bought herbs
and flowers which we potted on every step
to her apartment—intent
on making something grow.

Today, my son and his wife in Austin
are at a hospital for their first baby's birth.
My daughter and I talk by phone,
sharing excitement and nerves.
This time next week, I will make tea
for my daughter-in-law, on the sofa

with her baby girl. My daughter
will be miles away, at work; her tea
will be steeped in an auntie's jubilation,
she will drink it with generosity and grace.
My own cup, today, is cut—surprise to me—
with the tart flavor of tears.

This is The . . .

(for Jim on his 50th Birthday)

This is the infant, long-legged and thin,
who entered the world with a quavering chin,
who hung the moon when he was born:
this is the son that our family formed.

This is the baby, bald and stout
who soon as he could was crawling about,
touching and tasting his kingdom to own:
his favorite chew was the dog's Nylabone.

This is the brother, loving and sweet,
who ran to the car, baby sister to greet.
Together they played, make-believe running wild,
as pirates and cowboys—the life of a child.

This is the boy who set his alarm
and made it to school without any harm,
though he frightened his teacher, who called me to plead:
"I'm really undone—did you know Jim can read?"

This is the kid with a ball in his hand,
whether baseball or soccer he thought it was grand.
He bounced and he dribbled, he tossed and he caught.
Later on, it was hacky sack foot skill self-taught.

This is the teen who played the trombone
in marching and animal bands with good tone.
But he really stood out as a giant Big Bird
in bright yellow ruffles when the steel band was heard.

A Natural Helper, so named by his peers
for his calm, steady presence and listening ears;

political leadership, though, made him sore
when he ran 'gainst a buzzsaw named Steve Spoonamore.

This is the "Chirp"* who decamped to the south
and streaked through Scripp's dorms with a grin on his mouth.
He gave Black and White parties with buddies so fine:
he majored in math—and minored in wine.

This is the Price Waterhouse man, what a swell,
who as a consultant came under the spell
of a beautiful woman with "Husky-like" eyes:
Grandpa Jim led the cheers, claiming, "She's quite a prize!"

This is the marketing grad MBA
who landed at Intel and still's there today.
After nearly a decade of Munich's dark beers,
he and Jo returned stateside—they're wed seventeen years.

This is the husband with a partner as wife.
Together they nurture their children for life,
teach them compassion as worldwide they roam,
build community strong in their church and their home.

This is the seeker who tries many things.
When food, fun or travel come up, his heart sings.
By the Muse of Adventure he's clearly been kissed,
and his exploits succeed through his long To-Do lists.

This is the "Keeper" who's made us so proud
for fifty years now, and I'll say it out loud:
"I love you Jim, dearly, I'm delighted with you.
From this golden day forward, may your dreams all come true!"

* "Chirp"—a Pomona College student or graduate

October, Northwest

Sun streams

sideways

splitting atoms

into golden

energy.

Fog

whispers

slow down;

what you can't see

is still there.

Wind

whips

dried leaves

in flocks

like starlings.

Earth

tilts;

we fall inside

toward darkness

and rain.

Hello, Dalai

Robust, round-faced, red-robed,
he leaps to the platform,
places the finger tips of pressed palms
to his forehead, nodding
in our direction.

He settles on a delicate armchair,
plants bare feet in the oriental flower garden beneath it,
leans forward, one elbow on his knee
and confides cheerfully:
I don't have much to offer you.

He follows this with a full-throated
laugh, head thrown back in delight,
then delivers the very words
that comfort a friend the next day:

If you can't do anything about it,
        there's no use to worry;
If you can do something about it,
        there's no need to worry;
If you do all you can, and fail,
        there are no regrets.

The Dalai Lama is in town.
We shake our heads in wonder—
What a poem!

(Reflections on the Dalai Lama's visit, Key Arena, Seattle, 1993)

Out of Control, In to Life

Kayaking on the Salmon River,
I detoured over a waterfall,
hung for a splendid moment
bow up at an 85-degree angle,
then projected out of my orange torpedo,
plunged into the greenish, white froth
and tumbled over and over and over
in the never-never land
at the foot of the falls,
until I realized I might never get out.

Panic rolled with me in the bubbles;
a voice said *let go of your paddle*
and when I did, I
popped to the surface,
raced down the river's course
slammed into a guide's kayak
and was hauled to safety.

Hard, it was, letting go of my paddle
in order to live.
Necessary, it was, giving myself up
to the river
in order for the river
to save me.

How I Got Here

If you ask me how I got here
I might shrug and say, search me;
I might say
life's a mystery;
I might say
I walked through some doors
and not others;
I might say
now and then I get a glimpse
of the other side of my life's tapestry,
the side away from the slubs,
knots, and loose threads I see most of the time,
and that when I do,
 I sometimes think I see a pattern.

But all of these would be half-truths.

The truth—I know this now—
is that I was drawn,
as surely as the full moon draws the tides,
to the shores of some vast ocean
and that her depths, swells,
rages and exquisite calms
 are home to me.

If you ask me how I got here,
I'd say I turned one day
and headed home.

Appendix

Family Tree

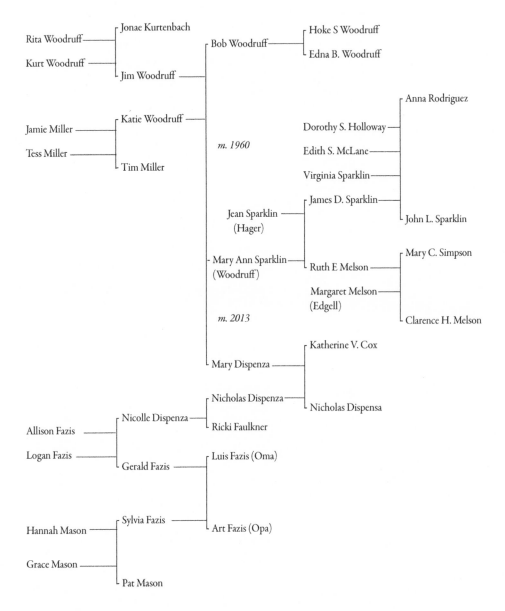

Rita Woodruff ── Jonae Kurtenbach

Kurt Woodruff ── Jim Woodruff

Jamie Miller ── Katie Woodruff

Tess Miller ── Tim Miller

Bob Woodruff ── Hoke S Woodruff
            └── Edna B. Woodruff

m. 1960

Jean Sparklin (Hager) ── James D. Sparklin ── Anna Rodriguez

Dorothy S. Holloway

Edith S. McLane

Virginia Sparklin

James D. Sparklin ── John L. Sparklin

Mary Ann Sparklin (Woodruff) ── Ruth E Melson ── Mary C. Simpson

Margaret Melson (Edgell) ── Clarence H. Melson

m. 2013

Mary Dispenza ── Katherine V. Cox

Nicholas Dispenza ── Nicholas Dispensa

Nicolle Dispenza ── Nicholas Dispenza
                 └── Ricki Faulkner

Allison Fazis ──

Logan Fazis ── Gerald Fazis ── Luis Fazis (Oma)

Sylvia Fazis ── Art Fazis (Opa)

Hannah Mason ──

Grace Mason ── Pat Mason

About the Author

Mary Ann Woodruff journeyed from her childhood home in Rochester, New York, to Mount Holyoke College and then Chicago before choosing a forever home base in the Pacific Northwest, which she has now enjoyed for more than forty-five years. Through poetry, Mary Ann celebrates people, chronicles events, and discovers her feelings. While more often recognized as mother, wife, volunteer, and organization development consultant, Mary Ann was always the poet, having participated in writing programs at Bellevue College, Flight of the Mind residencies, Hugo House in Seattle, and the University of Washington Writer's Program.

Woodruff's memoir, *The Last of the Good Girls*, was published in 2013. Skylark is a companion piece, in poems.

Mary Ann lives with her spouse, Mary Dispenza, in Bellevue, Washington. *Moon Day Press*, their book imprint, takes its name from their tradition of spending the day of each full moon together, delighting in explorations of the Pacific Northwest; the days usually include photography and birds.